CW00825641

WHATEVER YOU DO,
JUST DON'T

WHATEVER YOU DO, JUST DON'T

Matthew Stewart

HAPPENSTANCE

BY THE SAME AUTHOR:

The Knives of Villalejo, Eyewear, 2017
Tasting Notes, Happen*Stance*, 2012
Inventing Truth, Happen*Stance*, 2011

ACKNOWLEDGEMENTS:

Some of these poems, or earlier versions, have appeared or
are forthcoming in the following journals: *Acumen, Bad Lilies,
Finished Creatures, The Frogmore Papers, The High Window, The New
European, The Next Review, One Hand Clapping, Poetry and All That
Jazz, Poetry Birmingham, Poetry Scotland, The Rialto, The Spectator,
Stand, Wild Court.*

'La Vendimia' was included in *Ten Poems about Wine* (Candlestick
Press, 2023).

NOTE ON JACKET DESIGN FOR VISUALLY IMPAIRED READERS:

The background of the jacket is an old map of Extremadura in
Spain, where some of the poems are set. The collection title is
right-justified in large, black, lowercase letters, one word per
line, down the right-hand side, concluding about half way down
with the final word ('don't') in dark red. The author's name, one
word per line, follows after a gap, also black lowercase and right-
justified, slightly smaller than the title. No other text is visible,
apart from the tiny grey place names on the map. We also see blue
lines of rivers, red lines for regions, and black lines indicating
roads. Source details for this map are: Badajoz (Provincia). Mapas
provinciales (1893). Biblioteca del Instituto Geográfico Nacional,
CC BY 4.0 ign.es. The inside jacket features a monochrome OS map
of Surrey 1871-1872, sheet 030, drawn from Wikimedia Commons.

First published in 2023 by Happen*Stance* Press
21 Hatton Green, Glenrothes KY7 4SD
https://happenstancepress.com

ISBN: 978-1-910131-73-2

Printed & bound by Imprint Digital, Exeter
https://digital.imprint.co.uk

for Marina

CONTENTS

BRITÁNICO

LOS DOMINGOS

You've taught me to sip a *café solo*,
to let its bitterness seep through my gums
and mark the end of our tapas and wine,
just as you've taught me to relish silence
in the slow, shared sliding-by of minutes.

I no longer force the conversation
these never-ending Sunday afternoons
while muffled westerns blink on the telly.
An ancient carriage clock fights to strike four
and your mother pours her glass of water.

Perhaps this week she'll suddenly repeat
her suspicion of a neighbour's illness.
Or we'll sit here without the need for words
till your father stirs and cranks the volume
to signal kick-off at the Bernabéu.

VÁMONOS

It starts as a *Let's be off, then*
the first time I try to mouth it
across your parents' living room,
the minute hand wandering past
our scheduled time of departure.

It turns to a *Let's get going*
when I repeat it while you pause
for breath in passionate debate
over which of the town's butchers
sells the tastiest black puddings.

It ends up as a barked *Let's go,*
my voice on edge. We reach for coats,
grab the huge potato omelette
your Mum's made us, and hurry home,
another Sunday slamming shut.

HAY ROPA TENDIDA

'There's washing on the line' is a code
used only by adults at a pivotal point
in a conversation, just when someone's starting

to spill the juicy bits of their messy divorce
or their quarrel with neighbours. Hurriedly invoked,
it's a reminder young ears are listening in.

Everyone glances at the kids, who watch cartoons
as if they haven't soaked up every word. Talk turns
to the rising price of olive oil.

RENOVATION PROJECT

La Plaza del Concejo, Villalejo

We rip the bathroom out,
stripping the flaky walls,
and find a rough brick arch
hidden under plaster.

A blocked-up side entrance,
centuries old, it's set
to become our front door,
the building's lost stories

finding a voice again,
blending old plots with new.
Like my story with yours.
And yours with mine.

JULY PEAS

The pods are turning withered and yellow,
and the peas inside from plump to shrivelled.
They're running out of time, nights shortening,
moisture fading from the soil's memory.

We try to ignore their sudden decline,
shuck them, bin the ones that are too far gone,
give them ten minutes extra on the hob.
Pretend they're still as tender as in June.

CALOR

This isn't heat. This is *Calor,*
silting and clogging up the air.

It lies heavy in the bedroom,
our napes and pillows never dry.

Separate, clammy sacks of flesh,
we dodge each other's skin all night,

wake fur-tongued as if hungover.
The tap refuses to run cold.

Dogs are already cowering
in the shade by the time we leave

for work in air-conditioned cars
to spend the day at our office

ducking any slaps of sunlight
that make their way through gaps in blinds.

At dusk, we walk beyond the town
where henna-streaked soil stretches out

criss-crossed by tractor-rutted tracks
and strafed by rows of wire-trained vines.

A breeze ruffles the leaves. Grapes sway.
Our hesitant fingers meet.

LA VENDIMIA

After peaches come to an end,
before olives start, labourers
from over a dozen countries

head for Villalejo vineyards
and stoop and rise and stoop and rise,
grafting through the cool of the night—

snipping bunches, loading baskets
and heaving grapes into trailers.
By dawn, tractors have queued and chugged

their way through the winery gates.
Alchemy's about to begin.
The sleeping town will be woken

to heady scents of cherries,
yeast and just-crushed rose petals
wafting from roof to pavement.

TRANSLATOR, TRAITOR

The War was 39 to 45,
the suffering for the sake of a cause—
common enemies, common memories.

La Guerra, 36 to 39,
was brother killing brother, scores settled
with the neighbours, decades of reprisals,

memorials in every village square.
They only listed the fallen
from the winning side.

DRIVING LESSON

On the left...?
  ¿Por la derecha...?
My hand bangs
  against the car door,
forgetting
  which country I'm in,
groping for
  a quick change of gear
as if for
  something left behind
or lost
  between the two.

CARNET DE CONDUCIR

As you know, exchanging your UK licence for a Spanish one is one of the key actions for UK Nationals living in Spain to carry out before the end of the Transition period.
      —UK Embassy, Madrid, November 2020

The time I handed my UK licence

to Spanish civil servants

                my balance

tilted and swayed—

           I had to make a grab

for the counter.

        Two lives

               poised for decades

between two countries

          now reduced to one.

THE PALLETS

A 'third country' refers to any country outside the EU,
and in this case outside its economic structures—
the single market and the customs union.
        —BBC News, 14 September, 2020

Slouching on their fork-lifts,
the warehousemen watch me
trying to tell them why
40,000 bottles
must be shifted by hand

from normal, everyday,
fit-for-Europe pallets
to fumigated ones
they only used to use
for other 'third countries'.

I'm the one to blame now,
of course, *británico*,
a reluctant spokesman
for my country, supposed
to explain our folly.

ROLLING MY 'R's

Year on year, the Rs clambered
from the rasping depths of my throat
to the thrumming roof of my mouth.

Rojo, rollo y raro—
I still practise under my breath
in the shower or on the bus,

my tongue an exhausted flag,
stateless, buffeted, falling
short of the perfect roll.

WENDSDAY

Halfway through the word and the week,
my pen used to pause and stumble,
tripped up by my eight-year-old tongue

and even now I still delight
in having learned at last to swap
the *n* and *d* and add the *e*.

I stumbled, too, after coming
to Spain. Shook off routines and rules.
Let a new language soak through me.

Two more hassle-packed, tensed-up days
till *vino tinto y queso*
instead of cod and chips.

DAVID

I agonised for months over your name,
writing list after list of possibles
that were spelled the same in England and Spain
but with different pronunciations
to make you a native of both countries.

Instead, you've ended up being labelled
English in Spain and Spanish in England,
neither of us belonging anywhere,
always missing the language we've just left.
Me by choice. You by my choice.

CRAZY GOLF

David always asks me to go.
He loves the tunnels, bridges, ramps—
the mixture of skill and fortune.

We're even till the eighteenth hole
where my ball trickles gently back
down the slope again and again

and each time it reaches the tee,
I wonder who's lagging behind
on placing their latest order,

whose invoice is pending—and why
my pointless fretting never stops.
Never lets me simply play.

THE LAST CARRY

El Paseo Marítimo, Chipiona

You were seven and hadn't asked
for one in months, but the salt wind
had whipped your energy away
before *calamares fritos*
at our favourite place on the prom
left you woozy, slumped in your seat.

Even as I threw you over
one shoulder and braced for the trudge
to our house, my back was hinting
at a future without your breath
tickling my neck, at you walking
beside us, if we were lucky.

OUR BALL

A veteran of umpteen kickabouts
and scuffed attempts at the perfect free kick,
our ball's lived for well over a decade
under a rug in the boot of my car.
Loading the stuff you're taking to Uni,
I spot its faded yellow hexagons.

Impossible for me not to bounce it.
I pretend I'm lining up a curler,
and now you crouch as if ready to dive,
your grin escaping, playful, complicit,
till you straighten, remind me of the time,
and stow our ball again.

STARTING ELEVEN

Aldershot FC footballers from the 1980s

I

TONY LANGE

Released by Charlton at twenty
after barely going beyond
the reserves, he prowls our goalmouth,
a specialist in one-on-ones,
staring strikers down and waiting
to pounce as soon as they commit.

The board'll flog him off to Wolves
—a record transfer, *a dream move.*
He'll play the first two games for them,
making consecutive clangers,
then spend three seasons on their bench—
the best keeper we've ever had.

2

PAUL SHRUBB

Neat, precise and unassuming
in his haircut, passes and gait,
he times his tackles perfectly,

patrolling our flank as he's done
for years. If the fans cherish him,
it's because we can picture him

on Monday in an office
or warehouse or shop. At work.
One of us.

3

IAN PHILLIPS

Signed on a free transfer, shaven-headed
but for straw-blond sideburns, he's a throwback
to when defenders only defended,
to when the halfway line was their border—
no flashy attempts at overlapping.

All he wants is to play one more season,
one more season, his shoulder relishing
the chance to usher dainty right-wingers
straight into the advertising hoardings
if they dare to do him for pace.

4

MARK OGLEY

An inch too short to dominate
his striker when a cross comes in
(while filling in at centre-half)

and a yard too slow to shackle
his winger when he's one-on-one
(while covering as a full back)

his body stops him nailing down
a spot in the starting line-up—
no matter how much he wants it.

5

COLIN SMITH

He's come to us via Norwich reserves
and then a spell playing out in Hong Kong.

We won't remember him for his tussles
with strikers. Or for his perfect moustache.

It's for the FA Cup tie with Oxford
and the outswinger he leaps to meet

with a header that makes us believe
we'll beat this top-flight outfit.

6

ADRIAN RANDALL

His trademark's a slight drop of the shoulder
followed by a turn away into space
as he leaves the lumbering anchorman
from Halifax floundering in his wake
and measures up a skimming, arrowed shot
that has the keeper pawing at air.

Four years later I spot him on telly
when glancing up from my pint at a pub
in Manchester. He's bossing the midfield
for Burnley, still shifting up through the gears
with strides that belie his pace, still making
defenders fall for that same trick.

7

MIKE RING

He looks like a tennis player
or an import from Marbella:
elegant, perma-tanned and fast.
So fast that he's often the sub
when we're one down, minutes to go
and he streaks past shattered left backs
to snatch us our equaliser.

A disappointment if he's picked
from the start and gets caked in mud—
it saps him like everyone else,
no chants suddenly exploding
on the terrace to *Get Ring on!*
No way to turn the game around.

8

DAVID PUCKETT

I manage to buttonhole him
over my trembling, slopping pint
at the very first Fans' Forum.
No one has ever thrust their face
in mine like this to press a point
at the end of every sentence.

He speaks like he runs the channels,
words and elbows pumping with fire.
I quote some stat and his eyes burn
and he turns and leaves me for dead.
As if he's bearing down on goal,
slotting past the static keeper.

9

DALE BANTON

The first season I went,
he scored hat-tricks for fun,
less running than dancing
as he slipped his marker
and finished with aplomb.

That summer, York City
picked him up for a song
as a straight replacement
for their own top scorer
who'd just joined QPR.

Now—six long years later—
he's back, signed by the Board
to silence our protests—
though the manager knows
full well his legs have gone.

IAN MCDONALD

We love his knack for bringing long punts down
from shoulder height and playing passes blind,
weighing them so teammates never break stride.

Just as we admire the delicate chip
he placed precisely in the top corner
against Plymouth Argyle last Saturday.

Just as we understand the cautious way
he lifts his foot out of fifty-fifties
through the slurry of the centre circle

in remembrance of the vicious tackle
that smashed his ankle in the second game
after Shankly signed him for Liverpool.

II

IAN STEWART

Hiding from his teammates' passes,
this wisp goes through the motions

till those empty blue eyes flicker
with fire at a goading kick

from a defender on the nub
of his ankle. He'll square up

and get sent for an early bath,
or take the piss, beating him

and then going back to beat him
twice more—for the hell of it.

THE TWELFTH MAN

i.m. Simon Stevens

Forget stories, films and series.
Forget scripts and plots. There's only
one time we suspend disbelief—

an overcast Saturday
in March, standing among curses
and coughs on a crumbling terrace.

Our winger hoists a deep cross,
our striker buries his header
and all of us erupt.

FAMILY MATTERS

GRECIAN 2000

Mum said he only used it once,
the year I was born.
Fighting the tag 'an older dad',
his trumped-up auburn shone
in all my baby photographs.

So what if he *did* kayak with me,
dig an allotment,
lay a lawn and its paving slabs,
swim and roller-skate,
teach me a two-handed backhand?

I learned to mention his white hair
every chance I got,
felt a coward and a winner
when he lowered his eyes
and suggested, 'Ash blonde?'

TOUCH-TYPING

She took on piecework one summer,
sat at our kitchen table
in a secretarial stance,
shoulders spirit-level straight,
and turned into more than my Mum.
Her fingers danced to rhythms
of rattles and pings, to steel keys
hammering ink on paper.

When I upped and left for uni,
her routines were dismantled.
At sixty-one, she found a job
as dentist's receptionist.
Overwhelmed by printers and disks,
by rebellious keyboards
that mocked the sureness of her touch,
she lasted half a morning.

FULL CIRCLE

I haven't attempted
to be just like my Dad
for over forty years

so when I'm ironing,
pouring a cup of tea,
shaving or driving home,

I'm shocked to catch myself
singing the same jingles
and terrace chants as him,

imitating his tone,
adopting his cadence.

BANANA

Come to think of it, she didn't tell us
who'd got hold of the banana, or how,
and we forgot to ask, stunned by the news
that at ten years old she'd never seen one.

She was still proud her class had raffled it
for the war effort, still slightly mournful
at it turning black on her teacher's desk
long before they drew the winning ticket.

She wouldn't talk about gas masks, the Blitz,
the doodlebugs (how they changed to V2s)—
but she always recalled her fury
at the waste of bloody good food.

PAPER CLIP

Birth and marriage certificates,
recent passport applications,
their wills and the deeds to the house—

she slides a brand-new paper clip
over the top, under the base,
and forms a perfect rectangle.

How it brings their things together.
How neatly, temporarily,
it brings them together.

HEADING FOR THE AIRPORT

The cab suddenly turning up
twenty-seven minutes late
after my ten frantic calls
from the pavement outside your block,
your dressing-gowned silhouette
hovering on the balcony
with a halo of wispy hair.

My suitcase thrown in the boot,
doors slammed, the driver crunching gears,
I forgot our goodbye wave
while checking my flight. If only
that cab had left me behind,
longing for Spain. No way to know
I'd never see you alive again.

THE DRINKS CABINET

It smells of a not-to-be-repeated
attempt at unpronounceable cocktails.

Of a grandmother's sworn-by remedy
for a nasty cold.

Of a first visit
from some posh prospective daughter-in-law.

Of inappropriate leaving presents.

Talking of leaving—it's been left behind.
Left to me.

Left with bottles queuing up
for landmark-laden toasts
we never made.

Never will.

OPENING THE BOX

The music box tinkling a final note,
its lid opens with a puff of dust.

A pair of 5D London bus tickets
inside, torn and brittle to the touch.

Nobody left to say why they were kept,
where they started, where they once headed.

SARSONS, 568 ML

Stored in your cupboard for decades,
this malt vinegar has strengthened
while waiting for a battered cod.

Squat-shouldered, the bottle's bossing
my ketchup, reeking of chippies,
flaunting its 70s label

as if pints could dare to defy
their decline to half a litre.

'THE ARISTOCRAT OF PIPE TOBACCO'

Grandad's favourite. Its slogan decorates
the lid with those perfect ten syllables
as if smoking could somehow give you class.

Dad kept this tin of Gold Block in his shed
and filled it with discarded Allen keys,
rigid lumps of Blu Tack, dried-out biros.

I dumped the contents, using it to store
my memory sticks, though I've spotted
David eyeing it up already.

VALUATION

Mum rescued them from Uncle Percy's place
the morning the House Clearance Team arrived,
a hotchpotch of countries and currencies
that had disappeared before I was born.
I deciphered the faded names and dates—
they'd be worth a fortune!

I took them to a valuer last year.
They clattered out of their velvet draw bag
and he squinted at them through an eyeglass.
Collectors, he told me, only want coins
in mint condition. He could take them though,
sell them for their silver.

That was when I decided to keep them.
The places they've been to! The crimes witnessed!
Wines purchased, toasts made! Daydreams abandoned!
Debts settled, bets lost! Rough round the edges,
battered, used by umpteen people—we've got
more and more in common.

NUMBERS

The combinations for bike locks.
A girlfriend's ring and shoe size.

Landlines, postcodes and dates of birth.
The reg on Mum's old Escort.

They wake me at the strangest times.
I whisper them to myself,

let their echoes flow through my head,
holding on against the ebb.

ANNIVERSARIES

Tripping me up on an urgent order
or a best-before-date for a sandwich

like Mum's birthday tripped Dad up and forced him
to bluff, *But every day's your birthday here*

like I always chat to their ghosts at lunch,
every day an anniversary here.

MAP

Musty, coffee-cup-stained and frayed
    at the folds, your map was laid
across the dining room table.
The walks you planned were circular—
no retracing of steps for you.

I hunt down routes you never tried,
    adding to stains, cup by cup.
I prefer a zig-zag path though,
new angles and fresh perspectives
when I head back the way I came.

RETRACING STEPS

AVELEY LANE

Lights turned on but the curtains not yet drawn
in the dusk that lingers over hedges
and scrubland bordering Langhams Rec. Here's
the overgrown shortcut to the Bourne Stream,
the high wall that protects the vicarage.

Here's another mother getting supper
in Neil's kitchen. Here's another father
parking his car in Adrian's driveway.
They go about their family routines
as if they'll never be replaced.

THE GHOST OF TIM WALKER

What scared me was that *nothing* could scare you.
I joked and joshed my way round the hard lads
in class, managed to undermine their taunts.
Kept clear of you, though—ever since the time
you went at Mr Mason with a bat
for telling you it was your turn to field.

Your death's all across this week's local rag
and I wince when we're driving past the rail,
its V-shaped dent where your souped-up Fiesta
took a header down the river valley.
In the last seconds before impact
were you scared?

'MY HEART WILL GO ON'

Last month, across a haze of steam
and booze and sweat, you belted out
to perfection that piece of crap
from *Titanic* and you became
Celine Dion. It took me back
to our wedding day in Farnham
at St Thomas on the Bourne.
Hearing your Mum say *I do*
instead of you.

GOSTREY MEADOW

Showing my son round, I notice
a father taking a picture
of his wife and son who's melted
half an ice cream on his fingers
and the other half on his face.

It's a copy of a photo
in our album. Same river.
Same heat-laden sky. Same roles.
Same spot on the bank. Same pose.
Our trees were ten feet shorter.

SHORTHEATH ROAD

On the way to a relegation clash,
I stop at our local shop (now a Spar)
to get a pasty and Mars for half-time.

The freshly elderly form a neat queue,
updated versions of my Mum and Dad.
Damart trousers, Dannimacs, sturdy shoes.

Back at the car, I reach for my glasses,
prodding at grey that seeps through my sideburns
like moisture through tissue paper.

First gear, and I'm away.

AFTER THE REFERENDUM

24 June, 2016

Every greeting from the neighbours,
every question over a pint,
every pause in conversation.

I tell myself nothing's changed,
remind myself nothing's wrong.
Everything's changed. Everything's wrong.

WARNING

Just don't raise your voice if speaking
Spanish while on a bus or train.

Just don't think anyone means you
when they slag off the foreigners.

Just take no notice of the flags
in every town.
                Just don't wander

from my side at passport control.
And whatever you do,
                just don't

mention the B word down the pub.

FOREIGNER

My accent still reeks of Surrey,
so you'll assume I'm British.
That's what my passport says.

But there's a lift of my eyebrow,
rise in my tone at the end
of words. My dancing hands.

I wear these clues, can't take them off
like some disguise. I'm different.
Are you afraid of me?

FARNHAM LIBRARY CARD

After decades in my wallet,
you still survive my monthly cull
of receipts and jotted numbers.

You led me round a Georgian maze,
floorboards squeaking in the silence
while I hunted Shutes and Macleans,
Bagleys and Kyles—any cover
that seemed promisingly seedy.

Your yellow edges remind me
that my need for book after book
after book is tattered and frayed

and resolute.

SUSSEX BY THE SEA

On the dead-end road to the shingle beach,
past boarded-up pubs, graffiti-ed street signs
and empty pavements, I retrace our steps.
Parking in a mass of gravel and mud,
I pace alone along a patchwork strip
that does its best to be a sort of prom
while slowly crumbling into the foreshore.

Forty-two years ago, from the back seat
of our new silver Cortina GL,
I looked out at the churned-up, frothing sea,
the gulls and the spick-and-span bungalows.
They're still here despite their flaking paintwork
and tarmacked-over gardens. How much has
really changed? How much have I?

ABOUT THE AUTHOR

Matthew Stewart lives between Extremadura in Spain
and West Sussex in the South of England. He works in the
Spanish wine trade as a blender and exporter. His blog site
'Rogue Strands' is a respected resource for poetry lovers, and
he reviews widely for a range of publications. His first full
collection was *The Knives of Villalejo* (Eyewear, 2017). Before
that, there were two pamphlets from Happen*Stance*:
Tasting Notes (2012) and *Inventing Truth* (2011).